My Journal

_____

LOVE

POETRY JOURNAL

Poetry by KAS Sartori
Design by William Withrow

KBW CREATIVE PUBLISHING
LOS ANGELES

Another Book by
Kas Sartori

The Chosen Shell

LOVE, Poetry Journal
is a book of poetry by Kas Sartori with journal pages
Design by William Withrow
Published by KBW Creative Publishing
First Edition September 2024
Copyright 2024 by Kas Sartori,www.kassartori.com

ISBN 979-8-9918187-0-4

Dedication

For all those, whatever age,
who dare to take the necessary risks
to open their hearts to love.

Poetry

expresses our deepest, most profound emotions.

Stringing words together and laying them down in this
journal daily, weekly, monthly, or at random, can illuminate
our feelings, our struggles, our ever-changing life paths.
Plus, playing with words and their special meanings can be
a magical experience! By reading the poems in this book,
and then free-writing our own thoughts and poems, we'll
come to know ourselves better, the gifts of love in our own
lives, the straining of our hearts, and the steps we're willing
to take to risk finding love.

Love

a word with infinite meanings.

Read my poems, then sift through the words on the next page
and recall the Loves of your life. Remember what inebriated you
with the joy Love brings! Record also the myriad emotions Love
foisted upon your heart over the years. Did you shed tears for
a lost Love? Did you discover another, more precious Love years later?
Journal, play with these love-words, and create precious memories
of those exhilarating and tearful moments!

Affection   Best Friend

Yearning to Connect   Love of My Life

First Love ❧ Attraction ❧ Amusing ❧ Synchronicity

Passionate ❧ Fascinating ❧ Respectful ❧ Intimate

Soulmates ❧ Heartbreaker ❧ Beloved ❧ Jilted

Admiration ❧ Infatuation ❧ Sweetheart

Magical ❧ Fire ❧ Faithful ❧ Caring

Appealing ❧ Romantic ❧ Tryst

Heat ❧ Fierce ❧ Tender

Fling ❧ Intense

Flame

Window

A Window Has Opened...
And You're Not Asking More of Me
   Except
To Venture Out With You
                    And See...

                    KAS

Unbelievable Bridge

A bridge between two mountains,
a crossing urging me
to risk, to feel,
then whisper
what you mean to me.

The mask is now discarded,
My thoughts somehow are known
Pretense is all forgotten
Is this a journey. . .home?

My words that once were silenced
are coursing through my veins,
my thoughts, my dreams, my worries
flung open to your gaze.

How is it that you know me
in this strange, unspoken way?
You're bridging all my spaces,
I'll never turn away.

KAS

Imagination

Imagination

Imagination

Imagination

Sun/Fire

As if the Sun

Coursed Through My Body

   Warming

   Burning

   Every Inch of Me,

Until it Seared

Through Secret Inner Spaces

   To Fire My Soul

...And Make Me Whole.

                 KAS

Sandpipers Frolic

I arose from sleep,
    a night of potent passion,
pulling bright white curtains back
    to find a pale pink blush as far as I could see
    inebriating
        the sky
        the expanding sand,
        an ice-blue ocean,
        and a ring of tiny houses,
            their windows reflecting dawn.
From behind, your arms enfolded me,
a warm thrill streaking through me once again.
Together, we watched
    sandpipers play
    skittering across wet sandy puddles
    amidst the silver-blue surf.
    I wondered: Are they celebrating our new love?

                        KAS

Free-Write

Free-Write

Free-Write

Free-Write

Waiting

I Ache
  To See You
  To Talk
  To Touch You
Do You Understand
  That Any Waiting
Is Too Long?

KAS

Ocean

Waves Crash Against the Rocks

...Incessant Molding

...Relentless Carving

The Power of the Will

  Over Impossibility

KAS

Journal

Journal

Journal

Journal

Open Door

An Open Door

Inviting in the Risks

Of a Relationship: Elation............Pain

Friendship......Confusion

Sharing..........Silence

Whether the Door

Swings Wide Open or

Slowly Closes,

Would You Agree?...

The Worlds We Unlocked in Each Other

Challenged

A Growth Beyond our Expectations.

KAS

Full Moon Rising

Oh, full moon rising,
I could've glimpsed you on special nights,
every month, or every year.
Yet so many elements came together,
extreme currents of wind and weather,
hiding you away, depriving me of your warmth,
your light.
Not unlike the barriers and betrayals we commit,
the heartaches and regrets that distance us from love—
so we see only darkness
    for too long.

But one month, one week, one special night,
we gaze up to find the steadfast moon again,
beckoning us,
reminding us
that love does not die because it's hidden.
Covered yes, by separation, time and miscommunication
but never lost for good…instead
forever glimmering,
and waiting in enduring light
with forgiveness.

           KAS

Word-Play

Word-Play

Word-Play

Word-Play

UnEnding

An indestructible crossing,
rock-hard, rock-solid
the bridge we built between us
so many years ago.
Could I foretell or even fathom
it would last so long?
No, not then,
we ended it,
wandering off forever,
far away and far apart.
But now
I've circled back to you
reaching out again,
And there you are, circling back to me
bridging endless years
How can this be?
We're suddenly connected
        entangled even more than before.
Rock-solid
            Indestructible
                    Everlasting
                        KAS

LOVE'S Mystery

His gaze, his taste,
  his voice, his touch
Mesmerize me
He cares so much...
He makes me laugh
                  and love,
He makes me feel magical!

KAS

Poetry

Poetry

Poetry

Poetry

DISCOVER

THE MAGIC OF WRITING

Whether you love to write or not, I predict this journal will entice you to imagine your own memories and feelings about love. Then, with your laptop or pen, you'll kickstart your own unique muse.

Select a poem from this book. Read it and reread it, then...

Free-write: On a blank page, jot down a few Love-words from page 11. Add your own phrases. Fill the page with your random musings.

Imagine & Word-Play: Picture a memory. Choose a phrase or two to paint that scene. Pick more words to express your feelings.

Journal & Poetry: Stop and breathe. Read your creation. Add more phrases. Read it aloud. It doesn't have to be perfect! This is your own precious poem.

When your paragraph or poem is finished, add it to the LOVE journal.
You'll be surprised at the secrets your writing will reveal to you!

How Do I Love Thee?

How do I love thee? Let me count the ways
I love thee to the depth and breadth and height my soul can reach,
when feeling out of sight
I love thee to the level of every day's most quiet need,
by sun and candlelight...

Elizabeth Barrett Browning

Made in the USA
Las Vegas, NV
21 April 2025

21110935R00033